I want to be a teacher!
I say daily while growing up.

My family tries telling me to do other things.
They say...

4

WHY TEACHING?

Dedicated to everyone everywhere who still wants to be a teacher in order to inspire others.

They say nobody is a teacher anymore because...

...it is different than what it used to be.
...there are plenty of other jobs you should pursue or consider.

6

I want to be a teacher!

on TUESDAY
on NDAY
What about a software engineer?

9

on
WEDNESDAY
What about a project manager
or supervisor?

11

on THURSDAY
on WEDN...
What about a
lawyer or a judge?

13

on
FRIDAY

on
THURSDAY

on
WEDNESDAY

What if you became a digital artist or graphic designer?

art
technology
math
science
music
I want to be a teacher!
health & wellness
reading
social studies
language arts

on
SATURDAY

on FRIDAY

on
THURSDAY

on
WEDNESDAY

What about a realtor?
FOR
SALE

16

17

on SUNDAY
on SATURDAY
on FRIDAY
on THURSDAY
What about a physical therapist or a mental health therapist?

18

I want to be a teacher!

After weeks of similar conversations, my family finally asks:

WHY TEACHING?

I answer with:

Mom always talks about Mrs. Westfall and how inspired she felt after leaving her class in kindergarten.

Dad always talks about Mrs. Sheblessy and how he learned to write sentences in her 1st grade class. He still remembers her perfect handwriting.

Uncle Rob always talks about how Aunt Donna remembers her 2nd grade teacher, Mrs. Messer, visiting her events outside of school to show support.

Aunt Lisa always talks about her 3rd grade teacher, Mrs. Gregory. She still thinks of her when telling time since she was the teacher who helped her learn about clocks.

Aunt Suzanne always talks about how much Uncle John loved Mr. Korn's 4th grade class – the fun songs they sang and games they played helped him feel loved through the laughter.

Zahra's dad, Andrew, always talks about his 5th grade teachers and the way they helped him feel supported in a big school with more students.
102
102

Zahra's mom, Kate, always talks about Ms. White in the Blue Wing at Greene School and how she still remembers those being her favorite colors. Ms. White was part of a larger team of teachers in 6th grade who helped her learn about a mini society, how to sell goods and services and the value of money.

Vivian's bonus mom always talks about feeling so insecure in junior high and how teachers helped her feel safe and calm during some of her most challenging years. One of the many amazing teachers in 7th and 8th grade was Mrs. Gartner whose choir class led her to love music and travel to Chicago and Europe, sharing her singing with the world.

Carolina's older cousin always talks about high school and how
Mr. Tinsley brought reading to life for them by teaching about
the deeper meaning behind songs, poems, and stories.
They juggled in one of their class presentations which led to
becoming a circus performer.

Vanessa's older sibling always talks about Mrs. Hromadka, Mrs. Juenger, Mr. Veraldo, and Mrs. Hevia and how they encouraged a love for Spanish. This changed their life and inspired them to major in Spanish, travel to Spain, become a Spanish teacher and even bring their own students to Spain.

Paula and Tim always talk about their parents – Ms. Webb and Dr. Mott – who grew up in different states, both became teachers, then traveled to London with other teachers to learn more about schools in other countries... only to meet each other, fall in love and have their love for teaching turn into a love for one another.

This was because of teachers who inspired a love for learning about the world and a deep appreciation for travel.

I guess what I am trying to say is that it seems like every single job and person has been impacted by a teacher. Teachers have such a strong influence on society. I hear adults speak about their teachers in ways that have inspired them. I also feel inspired every day when I go to school because of the incredible teachers I currently have.

So, why teaching?

Because I, too, want to make a difference in someone else's life. I want others to look back and remember my class and the way I made them feel. While every job is important, I want students to know they matter and I want to help be part of the lives of my students daily.

SCHOOL

This is why I want to be
a teacher.

Jen Mott, Ed.D.

Jen Mott, Ed.D. is the author of this picture book, which included stories from her own school experiences.* A proud daughter of two educators, Dr. Mott & Ms. Webb (sound familiar?), Dr. Mott is also the author of Teacherverance, a non-fiction book about her research on teacher perseverance and why teachers stay.

In addition to writing and sharing stories to inspire future, current and former educators, Dr. Mott also juggles other roles as a full-time educator and an actual circus performer. Dr. Mott engages crowds of all sizes as a professional speaker and juggler, balloon artist, stilt-walker and fire performer.

From students to staff to large organizations and businesses, she finds inspiration in merging her passions for entertainment and education by helping motivate others to become the best versions of themselves and try new things. While based in Cincinnati, OH - Dr. Mott's love for travel takes her anywhere she can meet new people! Learn more at www.DrJenMott.com/books

Yes, all those memories are her own real stories and experiences plus she had each teacher mentioned in the book for at least one school year!

Sara Relojo

Sara Relojo is a children's book illustrator, mom of two, and longtime prekindergarten teacher who finds inspiration in the magical chaos of teaching young minds. From singalong story times to navigating little people's big feelings, her illustrations are born from real life experiences with a heavy dose of imagination. Relojo enjoys all types of media, but drawing is her first language and biggest love. She resides in Lexington, KY with her loving family.

Acknowledgments

Published by Dr. Jen Mott, LLC

Inspired by amazing teachers everywhere

Written by Jen Mott, Ed.D. - www.DrJenMott.com

Copyright © 2024—Dr. Jen Mott, LLC
All rights reserved.

Illustrated by Sara Relojo

Designed and created by Emily Hunter-Higgins - CreativeSnug.com

ISBN:
979-8-9899933-2-1   Why Teaching? Paperback
979-8-9899933-3-8   Why Teaching? ebook